PARENTING
Through
GRIEF

The Attunetion Approach

BY: Jade Richardson Bock
&
Craig Pierce Ph.D.

ISBN: 1497450268
ISBN 13: 9781497450264

Parenting Through Grief: The Attunetion Approach

Dedicated to the families who shared their
stories to shape this book, and
to many hundreds more who have shared their stories
to give and receive support at the
Children's Grief Center of New Mexico.

Acknowledgements

This book is a collection of stories and wisdom gathered over the years from families like yours and mine – families shaped by the loss of a loved one. Like all of the strongest kinds of help, it comes from many hands and hearts. Greatest of thanks go to the following men and women, who deserve very special recognition:

Kelly Geib-Eckenroth and Barbara Fries, LPCC are program coordinators at the Children's Grief Center. They both contributed beautiful stories, advice and experience to these pages.

Courtney Custer, LMHC and Nathan Hoge, Creative Director of Southwest Family Guidance Center participated in the nuts and bolts planning and final execution of the book's production.

Dr. Craig Pierce, pioneer of the Attunetion Approach, community visionary, wise counselor and a fully-grown bereaved child, made this project possible with his numerous contributions of talent and treasure.

Warmly,

Jade Richardson Bock

Table of Contents

What is The Attunetion Approach?

The Attunetion Approach is based on tuning in to what's important to you and your family, and then using three simple steps to create that within your family.

Dr. Craig Pierce originally developed Attunetion˚ as a parenting approach in his first book <u>Parenting Without Distraction: The Attunetion Approach</u>˚. The premise of that book is that in order to raise happy, healthy, responsible children, you need to pay attention and tune in to the right thing, at the right time, and in the right way for you and your kids. These three steps: Right Thing, Right Time and Right Way, can be applied to any corner of your life, helping you to create more positive relationships at work, at home, and in every aspect of your life.

In this book, we will be using the Attunetion Approach to help you understand grief and help you parent successfully as you grieve. The fog of grief can make both everyday tasks and major decisions seem impossible. The Attunetion Approach can help you get clarity around what matters most to your family. By paying Attunetion during your grieving process, you will be able to take concrete steps towards parenting with greater confidence, ease and love.

For a more in-depth look at the Attunetion Approach, please check out <u>Parenting Without Distraction: The Attunetion Approach</u>, which provides both inspirational insights and practical advice to parent in today's highly distracted world.

CHAPTER 1

Talking To Children About Death

> Myth: Children are fragile and need to be protected from the pain of loss associated with the death of a loved one.
>
> Fact: Children are resilient and, with honesty and compassion they can handle the finality of the death of a loved one.

"When is Daddy coming back from heaven?"

Annie called the Grief Center distraught. She was worried she had said something terrible to her five-year-old son, something that could not be undone and would confuse and hurt him deeply. "Two weeks ago, my husband passed away. He had been sick for nearly a year – colon cancer. Hospice was wonderful. He died at home, the way he wanted to. Last night our son crawled into bed with me and asked 'When is Daddy coming back from heaven?' I panicked! I didn't know what to say. I told him, 'I don't know son, I hope soon.' I couldn't break his heart again. What could I have done differently?"

There aren't any chapters in <u>What to Expect When You're Expecting</u> that cover telling children that their parent has died. We aren't given this information because in the "normal" course of our lives, we don't need it. About 1 in 9 Americans will experience the death of a parent before age 20; and 1 in 7 will lose a parent or sibling. That means about 90% of American's youth will not experience the death of a loved one – and our world is geared towards that 90%. (2009 The Untold Burden Study)

Annie loved her son deeply, yet her heart was battered. She didn't want to cause him any more pain. She thought the truth – that Daddy is never coming home again – would hurt him more than he could bear, so she chose to obscure the truth. Just for a little while. Just until he's old enough to handle it. Annie is not alone in feeling this way; many parents have been in the same situation. Unfortunately, the impulse to try and make the hard news easier to hear typically backfires because children grow and eventually learn that what we told them wasn't true. When that happens, we risk compromising their trust. We also risk compromising the feeling of safety we work hard as parents to give our children.

Explaining a death that has occurred

Because parents love their kids, it is natural to want to protect them from the pain of loss. However, we all do better when we are trusted with the truth and are given the opportunity to understand what is happening. What children dream up or imagine can be far worse than the reality they're facing. That's why simplicity and honesty are best.

- **Give concrete, clear explanations.** Refrain from phrases like "passed away" or "gone to heaven." It is important that children understand that death is permanent, that a person who has died no longer can feel or think, and that they won't be able to come back. "Daddy's cancer got so serious that his body was not able to heal. His heart stopped beating, he stopped breathing. He died."

- **Answer only direct questions.** Do not give more information than is asked for. Children will come back with more questions after they have time to process what you have already said.

- **Remind children that death is not their fault.** Children tend to be egocentric. As a result, it is important that you help them to understand that they did not cause their loved one to die.

Once your children begin to understand the permanence of death, then introduce them to your family's beliefs about the afterlife, if you choose.

By the Ages:

Little ones (ages 3 – 6 or so) may worry that their loved one, who is buried in a graveyard, gets wet when it rains or is afraid of the dark. Reassure them that when someone dies, they can't experience pain, discomfort, or emotions any longer.

We get into trouble when we start to look for an escape route from this hard conversation and when we fall back on euphemisms like "he's gone to a better place" or "he's in heaven now." These statements are not reassuring or comforting to young people. When we tell them their loved one is "gone" or "is" somewhere else, it sounds to them like their loved one has left and, more importantly, that this person has left them behind. We need to assure very young children that nothing they did (or didn't do) caused the death.

Very young children may say things like "My daddy died. Do you know when he's coming home?" This is an opportunity to go back to the beginning and re-explain what death means. Adult caregivers of bereaved children don't have this conversation just one time – you'll likely have it multiple times.

Older children (ages 7-12) still need reassurance. They need to hear that their loved one didn't choose to leave them; that they would be here if they could. Explain that death happens to all of us and when it occurs, we can't change it.

This age group may be more prone to worries that other people they love will die. Assure them that most people live a long time. It's normal for a child to lose a grandparent because they lived a full lifetime. It's still hard and we still miss them. It's less normal for a child to lose a parent or sibling, however. It's important to reassure them that it isn't likely they will lose another parent or sibling and, although your loved one has died, you're still a family and you can get through this together.

At these ages, young people are also likely to create a myth around the death of their loved one: "My mom said my dad had a heart attack, but I think he's really on a secret mission for the CIA and he's going to come back to us someday." Listen for hints about these secret beliefs and gently remind that the person we lost loved us very much, and wouldn't willingly leave us for any reason.

Teens understand that death is permanent and universal; however, they are surprisingly prone to believing that they may have caused or could have prevented the death. "If I hadn't slammed my door, he wouldn't have had that heart attack." Just as with very young children, teens need to be reassured that this incident was out of anyone's control.

Teens are in the midst of huge developmental changes. When a death occurs in the family they often are out of sync with everyone else's feelings. Yet, they want things to stay the same and for their loved ones to just "act normally." Sometimes teens take on mannerisms or habits of the deceased, trying to fill their role in the family. Dressing, talking, walking, behaving in ways similar to the person who died is not unusual and is part of the teen's process of coming to terms with a great loss.

Explaining a terminal illness or imminent death:

Most children become aware of death early on. They hear about it in fairy tales, see it in movies, or experience it with the loss of a pet. Yet death can be one of the hardest subjects to talk about with kids, probably because most adults are not comfortable with death or are struggling with their own sorrow. Trust that your children have the capacity to deal with the sad truth of death and handle it in their own way.

Even if you have not told your children that a loved one is dying, they probably know something is happening around them, even if no one says it out loud. Body language, worried looks, hushed discussions, telephone calls, relatives showing up, and the general sadness and tension in the adults around them give kids clues that whatever is happening is serious.

- **Don't hold back important information.** It is important to let children know that a loved one is seriously ill and may die. If the person dies and they are not told, they are left unprepared. Because younger children are egocentric, it is important to reassure them that nothing they did or said caused the death.

- **Children need honest and correct information given to them in a language they can understand.** For example, "Daddy is in the hospital because he is sick with cancer. It is nobody's fault. It is a different kind of sick than a cold or flu. You cannot get it from him. You can still hug and kiss him." Ask children to repeat back what you said so you can be sure that they understand and invite them to ask questions. Knowing that they will be kept informed about things that are happening will lessen their anxiety.

- **Children still need consistent guidance and boundary-setting.** Children still need parents to set limits. When parents are in shock and grieving themselves, setting limits can be hard. Others may say, "Oh... let it go; her mom is dying." Maintaining boundaries, keeping routines in place and keeping household rules intact, help kids to feel safe. Without the limits, children feel like things are out of control, which can make them feel insecure. Try to keep the schedule as normal as possible.

Visiting the seriously ill:

Visiting someone who is very sick can be traumatic, especially if children are not prepared in advance.

- **Ask first.** Before you take your children to visit someone who is sick or dying, ask them if they would like to go with you. If the answer is no, ask why. Once the matter is discussed, children will usually opt to go along.

- **Set expectations.** Let children know in advance what the person will look like, what the machines in the room are for, what the room will smell like and be like. Let them know if it's ok to touch or hug the person. You can suggest bringing a gift for the person or have them draw a picture or write a letter.

- **Measure time.** The visit should be relatively short. Ten to twenty minutes is long enough for a child of any age. Make time to debrief after the visit so you can address any fears or concerns your children may have. The most important reason for letting them visit is giving them a chance to say good-bye.

By the Ages:

At every age and stage, young people need a compassionate adult's guidance in accomplishing William Worden's first Task of Grief – to understand what has happened.

For young children, this understanding starts with the fundamental difference between alive and dead.

For older children, it continues with understanding how the loss of their loved one impacts others in their family.

For teens and young adults, significant life milestones (learning to drive, going on a date, graduating, starting college, and/or getting married and having their own children) are forever altered by the fact that someone they love is missing from these important events.

Everyone in the family is hurting and coming to terms with that hurt in his or her own way. Adult caregivers, while experiencing their own grief, can create an atmosphere where it's ok to talk about the person who died, to share stories, to wonder "what if" together, and to show emotions. For younger children, those emotions may come and go like clouds passing over the sun. For older teens and young adults, those emotions may feel overwhelming at times. Regardless of the ages and stages of the young people in your family, know that they can handle the truth and that each of you will get through this grief journey in your own time and own way, but always together.

Tuning in to what Matters Most:

RIGHT THING:

- It can be difficult to know how to help your children cope with the loss, particularly if you're also working through grief of your own. To help you focus on the right thing, begin by asking yourself a simple question: "Right now, what's most important for my kids?"

RIGHT TIME:

- Teach your children about death as soon as possible. It truly is a part of life. Animals, insects, pets, neighbors may die. Take the opportunity to explain the difference between alive and dead.

- If you are anticipating a loved one's death, talk with your children about what they can expect. Don't hold back important information. Be honest and use language they can understand.

RIGHT WAY:

- A child should always hear the news of a death from a family member with whom he or she has a close, loving relationship. And it's best that this talk take place in a familiar setting–preferably, at home.

- Be honest and encourage questions.

NOTES

CHAPTER 2

"Call Me If There's Anything I Can Do."

> Myth: Gently offering to help with "anything" is what people in crisis need to hear.
>
> Fact: When we're in crisis, we can't figure out exactly what we need, and often can't take advantage of help when it's offered.

"I honestly think that when someone dies, most people just don't know how to respond."
– Jessica, her husband Rob died by suicide

When someone we love dies, friends and family often step forward and offer help. "Call me if there's anything I can do" is a commonly heard refrain. However, as grieving adults we often have a difficult time organizing things and making decisions. The world is turned upside down and it's hard to know what to do, or where you actually need help. As a result, we don't know how to ask for help and we often don't call our would-be helpers. This furthers our own sense of isolation and feelings of being overwhelmed.

Sometimes our friends (adults and children) flee the scene. Many grieving people report coming out of the shock and the haze of the early weeks after the loss and realizing that their friends have seemingly moved on with their lives, leaving the grievers behind. This is another loss.

Jessica's story:

"My husband, Rob, took his life. His mother found him. When his brother called us, I knew the minute I answered the phone that something awful had happened. Rob had been in a very bad place emotionally and had threatened suicide for 18 months. We had gone to several therapists and also tried marriage counseling. We couldn't seem to get him the help he needed. I talked to my closest friends about my fears that Rob would hurt himself. They dismissed my concerns by saying he loved us too much to do that. He did love us and I believe he thought he was sparing us pain by removing himself from our lives.

We have two sons. Austin had just turned 5, Clay was 2 ½.

Friends and family were there for us that first week. There were things they could do – make phone calls, make food, make plans for a service. My closest friends came together and cleaned my house. The Tuesday after Rob died, I went back to work. I had to work – not only for the income, but for my sanity. I thought getting back to a routine would help me and my sons. That morning my best friend called me at work to check on me. I didn't hear from her again for 11 months.

I honestly think that when someone dies, most people don't know how to respond. At the time, I was resentful, angry and really hurt. I couldn't understand their behavior. I felt like I had lost not just my husband, but also my best friends. At the Grief Center, I met another parent with a similar experience. He said: 'Other people just don't know what to say or do.' I also believe our friends felt a great deal of guilt over Rob's death–the same Survivor's Guilt that I felt.

I did not, could not, know what I needed. People I thought were my friends didn't answer my calls for help. They didn't want to touch my pain. And so I was stuck in the pain of all of these losses for so long. Hearing that other people had lost friends after a death in the family allowed me to make some sense of what was happening and to understand it wasn't my fault. I ran into my best friend 11 months after she called me at work. I could see that she was so uncomfortable. Instead of being angry, I felt compassion for her.

What helped me to process these losses was writing. When you're grieving there are turning points, places where you struggle to understand. I needed to talk about what I was going through and what the kids were going through. Writing helped me to put those thoughts in order and to process them. I also connected with other widows on Internet forums. I was careful not to spend too much time in those forums – it can become consuming – but I did make some friendships that were helpful to me.

I still don't have a lot of people around me to talk too. I have reached out in the ways I know how. I often post on social media thoughts that start with 'Just for today...' These are my thoughts about Rob, his death, and what our family is going through. People who want to comment or connect often do – and they are very kind and supportive. Those who can't handle it don't, and that's ok.

I don't want to forget those turning points. After you lose someone you love, you are not the same person. Your priorities shift. You see the world with different eyes. I don't want to lose that experience. Otherwise, what was the point of going through this pain?"

Don't let grief isolate you.

In the beginning, you may not understand that a lot of people can't tolerate the pain you and your children are in. You may have a feeling of (or actually are) being abandoned by people in your life. It can be difficult to understand that people may avoid you simply because they are fearful of the pain you are experiencing. They may be so worried that something tragic could happen to them, as unrealistic as that is, that they avoid you. You may feel like saying, "Hey, my situation isn't contagious! Where did everybody go?"

In your mind, try making it ok that some people can't tolerate your pain. Maybe you'd be the same way if it were reversed. Who knows? The key is to surround yourself with people who make you feel heard and supported. Maybe you can even try a bit of humor with a friend and say, "I promise I won't have a meltdown if you come over, I just really need help getting my kids' rooms organized!" The point is, tell people exactly what you need and, if you can, let them know that sometimes all you need is logistical support, not emotional support. Let your guard down and accept offers of help. Remember, you always can say, "I don't know what I need right now, ask me again." It can often be six or more months after the death that you realize what you need.

Be specific about what you need.

In the haze of grief, it's hard to know what you need—and that can make it even more difficult to ask for help. Take heart; over time, you will learn to ask for and get the help you need.

One suggestion: Posting on social media a specific request can make it easier for people to enter your lives and give what help they can. "Can someone give me some ideas on how to fix my dishwasher?" might work. A word of caution though – sometimes requests for help go unanswered. Then, we must learn to be ok without it.

Support for your children.

As a parent, you still have to be attuned to what your kids need. They have their own grief that they need to process. They need normalcy, they need routine, and even some fun. Yet you may feel that you just can't do it all when it comes to meeting your kids' needs. When that happens, try calling a family member or close friend and asking them to help make sure you're not missing something important.

Remember, grief impacts how your brain functions, so you WILL miss details! Your sister may tell you that she sees that your kids could really use some new clothes and shoes. If you don't have the energy to go to Target and pick out clothes, ask for help. Most people in your life would be SO willing to provide assistance, IF they knew what to do. Don't be the person that says, "No, no, I'm fine, I can take care of it." Let them help you.

Call your sister or friend and say, "Can you please take the kids shopping for winter coats and some new shoes?" Chances are they will jump at the chance to help.

Tuning in to what Matters Most:

RIGHT THING:

- When it comes to the death of a loved one the world often feels as though it has been turned upside down. You feel out of sync, like your mind is disorganized and no longer working correctly. Guess what? You're right. You are in the fog of grief and your mind isn't operating in its usual way...and that is ok. The key is to name and normalize what it is you are experiencing so that you can communicate your feelings and needs with others.

- Remember, your friends and loved ones have no clue about how you feel, what you think, what you need and what you want. The only solution is to tell them.

RIGHT TIME:

- So what is the right time to engage the help of others? Simply put, the sooner the better.

- Put a support system in place as quickly as you can. Whether it's enlisting friends and loved ones to pick up groceries or run errands for you, bring you food, help with house or yard work, take your children to the zoo so you can have some alone time, or something as simple as driving you to a support group meeting.

- Getting help with these practical tasks can lift an enormous weight off your shoulders.

RIGHT WAY:

- While your friends and loved ones can't take away the pain of loss, they can provide much needed comfort and support. Let them.

- Look for opportunities to call on other's assistance. Get a loved one to help you create a list of tasks you need help with.

- When the next person says, "Call me if there is anything I can do," let them know what you need and be specific. We all handle tasks better when they are clearly defined.

- If you're not sure what you need at that moment, say something like: "I appreciate your support but right now I just don't know what I need. I know I will need some help in the future. May I call you then?"

NOTES

NOTES

CHAPTER 3

Going Back To School After A Death In The Family

Myth: School staff members are experts in working with children, even children in crisis.

Fact: Childhood bereavement is not addressed in most education and counseling programs.

"I was so disappointed in the school for handling a child's grief in such a thoughtless manner. Santiago's pain wasn't respected." – **Maribel, mother of Santiago, age 5**

<u>Maribel's Story:</u>

"**M**y son Santiago was barely five when his father died. He had a heart attack one night in his sleep. Santiago came into our bedroom and saw me crying and doing CPR. Santiago watched the ambulance take his father away. It was so hard on all of us. When he started kindergarten that fall, I told his teachers and the school counselor what he had been through. Santiago was a handful - he was angry, sad, confused. He didn't know where his Daddy had gone, and why his mother was sad all the time. For Christmas, the teacher had the students write letters to Santa asking for presents. Santiago asked for his Daddy to come back. The teacher sent him to the counselor. The counselor basically told him he had to write the letter asking for something he could actually have - and had him re-do the assignment. I was so disappointed in the school for handling a child's grief in such a thoughtless manner. Santiago's pain wasn't respected."

The death of a parent, grandparent, sibling or other loved one can throw a child into a tailspin of confusion. The child's feelings can bounce from sadness to anger to guilt and back all in a matter of hours. For parents and caregivers, returning to a regular routine is an important part of helping that child find his or her way in this new landscape shaped by loss.

One of the many issues parents struggle with is how to ease a bereaved child back into the school routine. When should the child return? How much should the parent tell the teacher? Who should tell the classmates? Sometimes these questions can create friction between kids and their guardians. Older children and teens may say they don't want anyone at school to know about the death. Often, they just want one place in their lives where they don't have talk about the loss.

A young man in a tween group at the Children's Grief Center lost his mother to breast cancer. He, too, wanted school to be a place where "things were normal" and begged his grandparents not to tell the new middle school he was starting about his mother's death. The school year progressed without incident until May. One of his teachers had the class work on Mother's Day cards. Facing his first Mother's Day without his mom was hard enough. Now he was in a quandary. He made the card. But then he took it to the bathroom and tore it into little pieces. His heart was broken, and he was filled with rage. That night he attended his support group at the Grief Center and said, "Those teachers are so stupid! How could they make us do that?"

A young person's desire to fly under the school's radar is understandable, especially when it comes to talking about death. Even well-intentioned adults can be susceptible to saying or doing insensitive things. Still, we strongly advocate that the adult guardian have a face-to-face visit with the child's teachers and school counselor and explain what has happened, and what the student's wishes are.

Not every school is well-equipped in dealing with the death of a student's parent or sibling. It's ok to suggest resources, ask questions, and be part of making a plan. Should the teacher announce the death in the class before the student returns and offer some ways for classmates to be supportive? Can the counselor (or another supportive staff person) offer the student an open-door to a peaceful harbor if they need to talk, or just get away? Can academic expectations be adjusted for a time? Does the school staff have experience in helping students cope with a death, or do they need to reach out to a place like the Children's Grief Center to learn effective tools?

The most important thing is ensuring your children have the support, compassion, and understanding of the school staff they interact with following the death of a loved one. To provide this, you must communicate with your child's teachers and school counselor.

It is important to realize that communication with your bereaved children is just as important as the communication with school officials. Talking with your kids about their wishes in terms of informing the school of what they are going through is a good starting point.

It is understandable that they may request you tell the school nothing. As pointed out in this chapter, many children want the school environment to be a type of safe-haven. They want one place where they don't have to think about or talk about their loss, a place where no one "sees" them in a different light, where they are not treated differently because they are grieving. Just as adults often see "work" as a place for "normalcy," children often see the school environment in a similar light–a place where things can be the way they used to be.

If your children ask you to not say anything to the school, find out why. Once you understand their fears and concerns, you'll be able to calm their apprehensions. For example, if they don't want the school to know because they are afraid their peers will find out and they don't want to be pitied or alienated, you can incorporate safeguards around that happening. In this instance, you might want to have a plan to inform only the teachers they interact with and their school counselors. Part of your plan would then include letting teachers and counselors know that you do not want your children's classmates to know what they are going through and that they should only approach the subject with your kids when it is absolutely necessary and when privacy can be assured.

Including your children in this planning process can be empowering to them and can help put their anxieties at ease.

Acting quickly is critical. In general, it is helpful for kids to return to school as soon after the death of a family member as possible.

If they are in the middle of the school year when their loved one dies, time is of the essence. Addressing the loss, and how to handle its effects in the school setting, needs to happen as immediately as possible. If the loss happens during the summer, you have a little extra time to prepare your children and the school for your family's new "normal."

Tackling the issue of school in a timely way will help ensure that your child has the understanding and appropriate support of the school staff; it also will help your children transition back to their academics and friends as smoothly as possible. The longer the school is uninformed, the longer your children will have to navigate their grief at school on their own. This could result in the unintentional but unfortunate "mishandling" of any "atypical" behaviors that may become apparent as a result of your kids' grief. Coming up with a plan with your children, and setting it in motion as quickly as possible, is the best way to help them navigate the difficult path of grief in a school setting.

Some schools are better equipped than others to help grieving children make the transition back to the classroom. Even if your school doesn't offer specific services, reaching out to the principal, teachers and/or the school counselor can give your children the best chance at a successful reintegration back into school.

Hopefully, informing the teaching staff of your child's loss will help in avoiding misunderstandings and insensitive comments. However, we know it is unrealistic to expect that your children will not have difficult times, regardless of our careful planning.

The loss of a loved one can feel like the end of the world. If, at any point, you feel the school and/or their staff is not equipped to compassionately accommodate your grieving children and their needs, it can be a good idea to reach out to professional grief centers. Grief centers can often provide support when it comes to working with schools and their understanding and treatment of bereaved children.

Visit www.childrengrieve.org. A National Center Locator will tell you if there is a grief support program in your community. Another great resource for grieving young people and their guardians is www.hellogrief.org. Additional resources can be found at the back of this book.

Tuning in to what Matters Most:

RIGHT THING:

- **Make a plan.** Involve your children in planning their return to school. Listen carefully to their needs and wants so that you can effectively communicate those desires to school administrators.

- **Talk to the school.** Make an appointment with the school principal and/or teachers and counselors to discuss your children's needs and wishes. Allowing your children to be present at this meeting can be a good idea. Some children will want to be a part of this to ensure the plan they agreed upon is communicated to their satisfaction. This can create a sense of ease. Other children will not want to be a part of this process; in which case, it is perfectly appropriate to allow them to entrust communication of the plan to you.

- **Brainstorm coping skills for when things are tough**. Your children will inevitably have some tough moments or days at school. Spend some time talking with them about things they can do to cope when they are having a hard time. This may mean talking to a special friend or trusted teacher at school, carrying something with them that helps them feel comforted or safe, or asking for time to go to the school counselor. To help make this easier, consider coming up with a signal or phrase your children can use when they feel the need to be dismissed from the classroom. Setting up a predetermined key phrase or signal for them to use with teachers or allowing them to call you from school can help reduce their stress of breaking down in front of their peers and can help to facilitate their immediate needs.

RIGHT TIME:

- **Collaborate with the school as quickly as possible for the best result.** Ask school staff for their suggestions on how best to re-integrate your kids into the classroom. Do they advise that your children return to school full-time or would it be better for them to return to school for just a few hours a day at first, gradually working their way toward staying for the full day? Can your children be given a break in the counselor's office after being in class for a couple hours as a way to allow them to rest and regroup? Sorting out these details early on will save added stress for you and your children later on.

- **Think ahead.** Work with the school to address upcoming lessons and events that may be difficult for your kids. As we saw in the earlier example, a simple heads-up about making Mother's Day cards in class would have given the tween's parent a chance to prepare the child for this upcoming activity and/or to have made alternate plans.

RIGHT WAY:

- **Encourage teachers to prepare.** If your children are ok with classmates knowing about their loss, encourage teachers to talk to students about what to say–and not to say–before your kids return to school. Similarly, talk with your children about what they may want to say to classmates when they return to school. Some children want to tell everyone;

others don't. It's important to let your children say as much or as little as they want. If your children are uncomfortable discussing the death with other kids, help them practice something they can say if questions arise. Also discuss with them how and when to talk with teachers if other children keep asking them questions they are uncomfortable about.

- **Make a communication plan.** Finally, encourage teachers to share their observations about your children. Knowing as soon as possible about any changes in behavior or performance can help your re-direct your children and provide extra support, if needed. If this is the start of a new school year, your children's teachers may not know them. If that's the case, encourage them to talk to your kids' teachers from last year to get a sense of how your children typically behave and interact in the classroom. It will be important that you and your kids' teachers and school counselors stay in contact in a way that works for all parties. Determine how often and in what way to keep in touch, such as through a weekly email and/or a call every few weeks, etc.

CHAPTER 4
What If The Kids See Me Crying?

Myth: It's bad if the kids see me crying; they need me to be strong.

Fact: Kids need consistency and safety but they also need honesty. It's ok if we show our emotions and share that we too are missing the person who died.

"Did we do something wrong? Should we have tried to make him forget his father?"
- Rebecca & Frank

Rebecca and Frank's story:

"Our grandson Christian was 18 months old when his father, our son, died suddenly. Our son was only 26 years old. Christian lived with his mother but would spend weekends and special times with us. When he was old enough to talk, we started telling him stories about his father and showing him pictures, especially pictures of the two of them together. We told Christian his father was in Heaven, and watching over him. One day we were talking with an old friend; someone we respect a great deal and consider to be a wise man. He told us we shouldn't have been showing Christian pictures of his father. He said 'Reminding him of his loss is like continuously ripping the bandaid off the wound – it will never heal.' Now Christian is five years old and he says he wishes his Daddy was here. Did we do something wrong? Should have tried to make him forget his father?"

Rebecca and Frank's friend was speaking with compassion to his friends, and with their best interest in mind. What he was saying makes a lot of sense from a logical standpoint. However, Christian's heart is not ruled by logic. He is a little boy who needs to understand where he came from, and what has changed in his family. By learning about his father, Christian will learn about himself. By sharing their love and grief over the loss of their son, Rebecca and Frank will forge a stronger connection with their grandson. In showing Christian that it hurts when we lose someone we love, but we can remember him by telling stories, his grandparents are modeling healthy grieving behaviors – which is just what Christian needs.

The family is usually our best support system when we experience something difficult. When someone in that family dies though, everyone is at a different place with how they understand the death and how they are coping with the ensuing changes. This can turn family members away from each other, creating more stress, more loss and it often ends up splintering the family apart. Spending time together often reminds family members of the person who is missing, and we're not sure how to deal with the pain of that loss.

Siblings may fight amongst themselves "You're crying all the time! Dad wouldn't have wanted that!" or "You're acting like nothing happened! Going on like our father didn't die! That's disrespecting his memory!" Adults and young people may want to talk about the person they lost, but they don't want to see the other person cry. So they change the subject, leave the house, pick a fight. Teenagers will often carry on like the death didn't occur, or conversely, try to fill the role of the deceased person in the family taking on their responsibilities or mannerisms. Adults are often in shock, then deeply grieving, finding it harder to make every day decisions or even remember where they put their car keys! Very young children don't really understand what has happened to their loved one. Everyone in the family is hurting, and expressing that hurt in different ways.

It's ok if the kids see you crying. It's ok to say, "I really miss Daddy. This isn't your fault, and I don't want you to be worried for me - of course we're all sad, and that means sometimes we cry."

Always tell the truth – in an age appropriate dose (for more specifics on explaining suicide and other complicated losses, see Chapter 9). The little one who asked "When is Daddy coming back from heaven?" in Chapter 1 needed to know that death is permanent, and that no one, no matter how much we loved them or they loved us, can come back to life after dying. To very young children we can explain the death in concrete terms, "His heart isn't beating anymore. He's not breathing anymore. He has died. He can't feel, or think, or laugh, or cry. We can though, and we will miss him very, very much. We can say good bye." Be prepared to re-explain and discuss the death (how it happened, exactly what happened) as the child grows and matures. As Fred Rogers said, "If it's mentionable, it's manageable." You can manage having these hard conversations in your family and, with practice, it gets easier.

What we don't tell them, they will tell themselves – and often the story they make up is far worse than the truth. If we don't explain to them in simple, concrete terms the facts of the situation, and especially that the death was beyond anyone's control and not anyone's fault, they may think it's somehow their fault that their person died. Even teenagers need to be explicitly told, "This was not your fault." Often, we want to find someone to blame – the doctors, the ambulance driver, even the person who died – but we must remind ourselves and our loved ones that often, bad things just happen. It's not fair, and it's not right. Our work is to learn how to cope with that, and ultimately to reinvest in life.

Taking Care

In times of stress, it's typical to put ourselves at the bottom of the "to do list." However, as the flight attendants tell us – we must put on our own oxygen mask before helping others. Move yourself up on that list. Take some time to care for yourself, and acknowledge that you are beginning a very difficult and life changing journey. Start a conversation with other family members about how each person will take care of themselves. Purposely schedule healthy activities for you and kids, that you enjoy, and that you will do. This is part of your work. The death of someone we love changes us forever. It is one of the hardest things we'll ever face in our lives. We must be gentle with ourselves, and our loved ones, as we venture into a new way of being – living with loss.

Tuning in to what Matters Most:

RIGHT THING:

- Start by tuning in to how you're taking care of yourself. Try to take a few minutes each day, or even a few hours, to pay attention to how you are feeling and what you can do to nurture yourself.

- Exercise, drinking plenty of water and eating well are more important when your body and mind are under stress than any other time. Set aside time to do these things for yourself, a little every day.

- Work on accepting your feelings, whatever they may be, and allow yourself to grieve. Sadness, loneliness, fear, confusion and anger– these painful emotions are a natural and normal response to loss. You can try and suppress them or hide from them but in the end, ignoring your feelings will only prolong the grieving process. By tuning in and acknowledging your pain and taking responsibility for your feelings, you can help avoid the complications that often come with unresolved grief, such as depression, anxiety, substance abuse and health problems.

RIGHT TIME:

- Give yourself permission to let the emotions of grief come and go. It's ok to be angry, to go to an open field and yell, to cry or not to cry. At the same time, it's also ok to laugh and to find moments of joy.

- Remain open to taking in the pain and meaning of death a little at a time. Your grief is your own and no one has the right to tell you when you should be "over it," or when to "move on." Grief takes as long as it takes to resolve itself. It is an intensely personal process that can't be measured by a formula or timetable.

RIGHT WAY:

- One of the most effective ways to express your grief is through some tangible or creative expression of your emotions. Try journaling, writing a letter expressing the feelings you wish you had shared with your loved one, creating artwork celebrating the person's life or depicting what you lost.

- Set aside time to do things that make you feel good or are comforting, like taking a hot bath, listening to music or taking a walk.

- Learn to accept that grief is hard work. It consumes a lot of energy and can be exhausting. For this reason, it's important to remember you can reach out and ask for help. Allowing others to be of assistance and to love you through this challenging time is a key to healing.

- Remember, if at any time the grief feels too much for you to bear, seeking guidance from a professional therapist can help you and your family take the next steps along the path of living and parenting through grief.

CHAPTER 5

Coping With Fears

Myth: Kids are generally happy-go-lucky and don't worry about the future the way adults do.

Fact: After a loved one has died, kids are typically very worried that similar tragedy will befall their other loved ones.

The Worry Tree activity at the Children's Grief Center — kids share their fears
"I worry that my dog will die." "I worry I won't do good in school." "I am afraid
someone else will die." "I worry my mom will die."

"I worry my mom will die." – **6 year old whose father died**

The unthinkable has happened, and a loved one is gone. Once the shock wears off, and the understanding that death is permanent and universal sets in, we often experience new fears to go along with this new understanding. Kids (and adults) have learned that our world is much more out of our control than we would like. Accidents happen. Doctors can't cure all diseases. People hurt other people. Suddenly life can be very scary.

William Worden, author of the <u>Childhood Bereavement Project</u>, followed 70 families with 125 children between the ages of 6 – 12 who had experienced the death of a parent. He found that four months after the death, 44% of them reported their greatest fear was that the other parent will die. A year after the death of a parent, 62% of the children were worried for their other parent. (<u>Children & Grief: When a Parent Dies</u>, William J. Worden 1996)

At the Grief Center, we often do activities around sharing our fears. One is called The Worry Tree. Nearly all children write that they are afraid of losing the other parent. They often have daydreams about what could happen to cause their remaining loved ones' deaths. Yet, they typically don't share these worries with their caregivers for fear of upsetting them, or causing more strife in the family. Regardless of what fears they do or don't express, the young people in your family need to know that there is a plan in place to care for them.

Adults have fears too. They find it scary to plan for the future after a spouse or child has died. Everything is different now. Our assumptions about how life will be have forever changed. No one can promise to "always be here" – we know that is not true. Help your children understand that their fears are not only ok, they are perfectly normal and shared by many other kids who have lost a loved one. Often kids can feel like they are the only ones who have these fears. It can ease their minds to know that other kids have the same scary thoughts.

Putting a name on fear:

What are some of the fears your children may experience?

- **Fear of losing a parent or other loved ones.** To a child, a parent is everything. When one dies, a child's fear of losing the other parent can become powerful and overwhelming. To deal with the intense fear of being left unprotected and alone, children may become whiney, never wanting to leave your side. Any time apart can become a source of tremendous anxiety.

- **Fear of abandonment.** The emotional trauma of losing a parent, sibling, relative or friend can spark intense fears of being left behind and abandoned. They may express fear of every day events like going to school or the grocery store. Physical symptoms like stomachaches and headaches may surface whenever your children are separated from you and want to return home. Bed-wetting, sluggishness and uncharacteristic forgetfulness may also be signs that your children are dealing with unspoken fears and unresolved grief and need attention and reassurance.

- **Fear of death.** When a parent or loved one dies, it's not uncommon for children to fear that they too will die soon. A child may wonder, "Grandpop died in his sleep. Am I going to die too when I go to bed tonight?" Death might be linked to a hospital, a car accident, a particular disease; whatever the cause of their loved one's death, they may develop a fear that they will die in the same way.

- **Fear of sleep.** Going to bed can make some children fearful as many equate sleep with death. A child who is afraid to go to sleep may ask to read book after book at night, cry incessantly, or prolong their preparations for bed. The fear of sleep may result in recurring nightmares, which further feed their fear of going to bed at night. As a result, sleep disorders such as insomnia are a common experience for children who lose a loved one.

- **Fear of showing emotions.** While young children typically display their emotions easily in the face of grief, older kids may become afraid to do so out of fear of saying or doing the wrong thing. They may feel guilty for making you cry and/or express anger at others for talking about the person who died. This can make it extremely difficult for a young person to process the powerful and often conflicting emotions of grief.

- **Fear of the unknown.** Death creates unimaginable upheaval in a family's life and the powerful emotions that come with this event can cause children to become afraid of everyday situations and events. Anxiety may set in along with undefined fears and generalized uneasiness that something terrible is about to happen.

Communication in the family is the key to wiping away worries. Let your kids tell you their fears and let them know that it's ok to feel scared or to cry. And it's ok if you cry when they tell you their fears. It's important for kids to know that they are not adding stress or worry by sharing their thoughts with you. Kids might hesitate to share their feelings unless they know this.

For older kids, share with them that you worry too and describe for them what that feels like. Sometimes sharing our fears is actually comforting because then we are no longer wondering what our child or parent is thinking. By being honest, you take some of the mystery out of the equation. This is especially important for younger children because their imaginations can run wild and their imagination is often far worse than reality.

Calming Fears

One mother shared, "If I am going to be late to pick my kids up, I know they will worry. When that happens, I call the school and insist they tell my children that I called and am on my way." This parent is using communication to alleviate her kids' worry so they know she is just running late and nothing bad has happened to her. Another parent said, "The first year after my husband died was the scariest. I was worried about everything; every phone call made me jump. I needed to know where my kids were at all times. Over time, that began to lessen."

As parents, we know all too well how much we worry about our kids. After the loss of a loved one, that worry can take on a whole new power. This is to be expected and will lessen over time. In the meantime, be mindful of what you can do to feel more secure. For example, have your kids call you as soon as they get home if you are not there, or ask the babysitter to call you every couple hours just so you know everything is ok.

For many parents, what helps is taking action. As difficult as it is, you must deal with the issue practically by putting in place a contingency plan for their care. If you do not have a will and life insurance in place, get one developed. If you had these created before the loss of a loved one, especially a spouse or a child, they will need to be updated to reflect the family's new situation. Be sure these documents name guardians for the kids, and if you feel your children are old enough, share this information with them so they understand what would happen to them in the event that you are not there to care for them. You must be able to tell your kids that there is a plan for their well-being. This will help make them feel far more at ease and will also relieve pressure from you because you can feel confident that there is a detailed plan in place should the unthinkable happen.

Tuning in to what Matters Most:

RIGHT THING:

- Pay attention and tune in to how your children are experiencing the loss. What are they feeling and thinking?

- It is common for children to fear the surviving parent's death. Tune in to this! Fear is a normal response. However, you can help calm your child's fears once they are identified. Reassuring them that they will always be cared for, and a plan is in place for them is a concrete way to help allay their fears.

RIGHT TIME:

- The time for communication with your children and planning for their safety and care if you were to die unexpectedly is NOW.

- Let your children know that it always is ok to share their feelings and fears.

- For smaller children or children who aren't very vocal, it is often a good idea to use drawing or writing to help them express what they are feeling and how they are experiencing the death. Picking different colors of crayons, scribbling with different intensities on a piece of paper can help them describe the strong feelings they may have.

- Let them know it is ok to cry and it is ok to say things that are sad.

RIGHT WAY:

- Plan, plan, plan! It is critical to have plans in place for your children if anything were to happen to you.

- Make sure you have updated your will, name one or more guardians to assume responsibility for your children if something were to happen to you, get life insurance if possible...and DO IT NOW.

- Then take the time to share the plan with your children. Your children need to know that they will always be protected no matter what happens.

NOTES

NOTES

CHAPTER 6

Secondary Losses

Myth: You don't really need to grieve secondary losses because they are so insignificant compared to the loss of the person.

Fact: Secondary losses are real and painful. Just like grieving the person who died, mourning secondary losses allows you to move forward and eventually feel hopeful about the future. It is not selfish or petty to feel these secondary losses and especially for children, these losses may feel even larger to them than the original loss of the person.

"I miss Sunday mornings. My dad would make pancakes. He died of cancer."
12 year old girl

It seems to the outside, non-grieving world, that the moment our loved one died must have been the hardest part. After all, that was the moment our lives changed forever. However, grievers know that's not the whole picture.

Alan's story:

When Alan was 17, his 24 year old sister Ana died by suicide. She was a recent college graduate, and a bright, creative, successful, beautiful young woman. Alan was a junior in high school. "When word got out of her death, many people came to our house. I retreated to watch Harry Potter for three days. I didn't want to talk about it; that wasn't what I needed.

Ana had attended a very prestigious college. I was applying to very competitive schools at the time. I continued to be successful in high school; I appeared to be doing alright. However, almost a year later, when I received an online acceptance letter and opened it, I immediately went from being ecstatic to sobbing a minute later. Suddenly there was this wonderful thing that I couldn't share with her. She would have been so proud. I printed the letter and took it to the cemetery, to my sister's grave. This was something I needed to do on my own. I know she'll never know my partner, she'll never come to my wedding…there's a litany of things I'll never get to experience with her.

It wasn't until my sophomore year in college that I wanted to talk about it. I found a counselor through my school to help me process my sister's death. I needed to meet some of my own goals before I was able to deal with the grief."

When Alan lost his sister, her death was stunning. Like most of us, Alan waded through the numbing, heavy feelings of loss. Then, as days and weeks go by, other realizations start to arise. The initial loss is great - we lose our loved one, and someone who loved us back. Then we realize that we have lost the ability to share with them our special moments, ask them for advice, rely on them for support. Sometimes we're confronted by the loss surprisingly; in the store we pick up their favorite treat only to be reminded that they aren't here to enjoy it. Suddenly, a simple trip to the grocery store ends in tears and frustration.

For young people, the impact of secondary losses goes on and on and on. It's a factor in how kids re-grieve the loss as they progress through developmental stages and gain new understanding of how their loved one's death is continuing to impact their life. Secondary losses can be like a pin prick in the red balloon of our special days. They can feel deflating. It can seem as though every joyous occasion is now clouded by the shadow of our loss.

C.S. Lewis, the man who gave us the <u>Chronicles of Narnia</u>, wrote another powerful tale called <u>A Grief Observed</u>. This book describes his experience after losing the great love of his life, Helen Joy. He describes what we are calling secondary losses in the following way: "I think I am beginning to understand why grief feels like suspense. It comes from the frustration of so many impulses that had become habitual. Thought after thought, feeling after feeling, action after action had Helen for their object. Now their target is gone. I keep on through habit fitting an arrow to the string; then I remember and have to lay the bow down." [C.S. Lewis, A Grief Observed (London: Faber and Faber, 1961), 41.]

Examples of Secondary Losses:

An 8 year old boy whose 12 year old brother was killed asked his mother, "Does this mean I have to do all of his chores?" This boy is not being selfish at all. It is developmentally normal for children to focus on details such as this and how they impact them. The truth is, this boy lost a brother, playmate, teammate, AND someone to share the chores. Here are other examples of secondary losses you may encounter:

- Loss of a role: "I'm no longer someone's dad, wife, sister, etc."

- Loss of a family structure: The family may now have one child/parent instead of two.

- Loss of financial contribution: The family now might have to survive on less income.

- Loss of attention: Especially for children, if a parent or sibling dies, there is one less person to play with them and take them places.

- Loss of a person's special role in your life: "Dad was the one who played baseball with me and now I can't play baseball anymore."

- Loss of community: If the family has to move after a death, everyone in the family loses friends, neighbors, classmates and other important people.

- Loss of self efficacy: You may feel that you have lost the ability to manage daily life, meet your kids' needs and attend to what needs to be done.

- Loss of a support person: "Grandma was my 'go to' person to talk with about friends. Now I don't have that outlet anymore."

- Loss of logistical support: If a parent was always the one who took the children to soccer practice and now the other parent has to work full time, there may be no one to take them to their activities.

- Loss of a partner in activities: "My husband and I played cards on Friday nights with two other couples. I can't do that anymore."

- Loss of faith, safety and trust: Especially when someone dies in a tragic or violent way, we question our faith. Our sense of security in the world is broken and we may find it hard to trust others.

- Loss of health and well-being: After a loss, health issues are common due to stress, lack of sleep, and emotional trauma.

The key to disarming the impact of secondary losses is to acknowledge them. Try to look at life from your other family member's perspective. How has the loss of the loved one changed the trajectory of your future? This is going to be different for each person in the family. Their relationship with the deceased was unique, and their experience of losing that person will be unique as well. It's important to recognize that "secondary losses" are a way of describing the incremental and sometimes surprisingly painful ways we miss our loved one. We lived a life together. Secondary losses, in their painful pin pricks and sudden realizations, slowly teach us that we can live that life apart from them.

Tuning in to what Matters Most:

RIGHT THING:

- After the loss of a loved one, try to identify for yourself what potential secondary losses might be for you. Then do the same for your children, since their second losses are likely to be different than yours.

- For example, if your spouse has died, you may be experiencing not just the loss of your love, but financial losses, the loss of a parenting partner, etc.

- At the same time, your children may be dealing with the loss of someone to care for them and play with them. Talking about the secondary losses will help you establish a new normal and adjust to life's differences after a loved one has died.

- Try to minimize the impact of the secondary loss by finding alternatives that could fill that need. For example, if the secondary loss is that Dad used to make pancakes every Sunday morning, what new ritual could your family create? Maybe you could still make pancakes on Sundays and talk about Dad as you eat breakfast. Or maybe you and your kids could visit their father's grave on Sunday mornings instead. The point is to create new rituals while also acknowledging the pain that the loss of the original ritual or experience created. Assess what you want to keep about the ritual and what you want to change – then begin to put the new practice into place.

RIGHT TIME:

- For many issues relating to grief, the right time to address them is usually as soon as possible. However, when it comes to secondary losses, sooner is not always better. Your family needs to feel ready to acknowledge the loss before they can move on to a new tradition or practice.

- Do not try to address every secondary loss at once, deal with them as they arise. The fact is that there will be secondary losses that you haven't yet considered that will show up days, weeks, months, or even years from now.

- Kids will bring up things in the moment in which they are experiencing them, so as a parent, STOP and tune in to your children WHEN they bring up an issue. That is the time to respond.

- Pay attention to when kids resist doing things they once loved to do. They may avoid activities that are too painful after the loss. Be attuned so that you avoid forcing them to participate in things they resist.

RIGHT WAY:

- Anticipate that secondary losses will arise and throw you back into the depths of grief even if you have been doing and feeling better lately. Expect that the people around you might be confused by this. As a result, you may want to explain to them why you suddenly appear to be acting as you did just after the death occurred, even though it is many months later. If the people around you understand why you are struggling, they may be more likely to offer support and less likely to withdraw or avoid you. As you move through these losses, be authentic about what feels right for you and your family. Remember, every person and every family handles secondary losses in their own way.

NOTES

CHAPTER 7

Milestones And Holidays After A Loved One Has Died

> Myth: It's important to maintain family traditions and keep as much the same as possible.
>
> Fact: It's important to acknowledge that things aren't the same, and it's ok to make changes, involving the whole family and keeping in mind what each person wants to keep and what they want do differently.

"It was December 15th when our daughter died – 10 days before Christmas. Our other two children were 5 and 9 at the time. We still had to make Christmas special. The oldest didn't want to talk about his sister's death; the other one, well, it was all she wanted to talk about." - **John**

Happy Holidays?

Due to the huge emphasis placed on family togetherness during the holiday season and other special days like graduations, birthdays, anniversaries, etc., we become even more acutely aware of the void in our lives left by loved ones who have died. There is no right or wrong way for how things should go during this time, but the more you plan ahead and start thinking about how to manage the impending celebrations and events, the easier it will be. We will be sad at times. We may even dread those special days we used to enjoy so much. What if, this holiday season, we made a little space for that sadness? What if, together, we acknowledged that someone we loved so very much is missing?

What if we found a way to remember that person with honor and warmth? What if, together, we talked about our special traditions, and made new ones?

Jade's story:

As I write it's October - the 18th actually. My holiday season begins today with my father's birthday. Next week is the anniversary of his death, and a new milestone. I was 17 when he died – and that was 18 years ago. He's now been dead for more years than we had together. My father was a commercial pilot and he was killed in a plane crash on October 27th on the small Pacific island of Saipan.

Halloween, a holiday he had already planned his costume for, was spent preparing for his funeral. I still don't remember Thanksgiving that year. I do recall flashes from that first Christmas. It was so empty, sad and, despite Micronesia's tropical clime, it felt cold. My mother made an American treat for our Christmas dinner that year – spaghetti. My newly shrunken family ate together in silence, and tried not to make eye contact.

Recently I spoke to a grandmother, who is now raising grieving grandchildren after the death of their mother, her daughter. I asked how she was feeling about all this. With a heavy sigh, she said she doesn't want to cry in front of the children because she doesn't want them to feel sad, and start crying too.

That sounded very familiar to me. "I don't want to appear sad, because I don't want you to feel sad." We're all sad enough on the inside, right? So we pretend there are no lumps in our throats or tears in our eyes. I think that's how my family felt, and I think those feelings ultimately had a hand in driving us apart for so many years after my father's sudden death. When we were together, we were unavoidably reminded that Dad was missing. Not that we ever truly forgot.

Individuals and families go through a myriad of emotional, physical and cognitive reactions during the holidays. They may feel guilt, confusion, anger or the need to withdraw and isolate themselves. Some people may turn to harmful coping techniques: excessive drinking, drug use, or aggressive and/or reckless behavior. Children are often confused about how celebratory they should feel. Little children are naturally excited about the holidays, in sharp contrast to older people's sadness. Other reactions include trouble sleeping, changes in appetite, difficulty concentrating, becoming clumsy or forgetful, or even suffering from panic attacks. It is important to recognize that these are normal and common reactions and to focus on becoming more aware that we are hurting and need special care during these harder-than-usual times.

The National Alliance for Grieving Children emphasizes the importance of facing the holidays with "intentionality" – meaning you are planning for holidays beforehand and developing strategies for coping. By having conversations and making plans early on, the emotions and energy surrounding the experience are then spread out over a period of time, rather than being concentrated all in one day.

You may wish to create a new tradition or stick to things you have done in the past. Remember that whatever you decide to do the first year, you are not obligated to do the same the next. Helping others in need could be a great way to take your mind off the grief that you are feeling yourself. Another idea is to plan a special celebration; it can be helpful to have something fun to look forward to. If things feel overwhelming, plan to call on all of those people who have said "if you need anything…" and ask them for help.

It is important to try to include any young people in your family in the holiday planning as much as possible. Talk about what traditions you want to keep, what you want to change, or what you might try differently just for this year. Assign specific responsibilities to each family member and consider doing a special project together to honor and remember your loved one and/or suggesting discussion topics to talk about as a family. A list of ideas for activities is at the end of this chapter.

At the Children's Grief Center, one thing we learn is that letting tears fall is actually not the end of the world. **Truthfully, the worst has already happened. That's why we're all grieving**. Allowing yourself to feel the feelings is ok. Kids are expert at this – they feel those hard feelings – and then they feel something else. Like a cloud passing over the sun, the pain comes and goes in doses just right for their size. They feel it, they acknowledge it, and then they go play. And the cycle continues. We could learn much from their bravery (the feeling and acknowledging) and then the "going on" to play. "Going on" doesn't mean we'll forget our special person. We'll never stop loving them or feeling the memory of their love for us, but (as I found printed on my tea bag at lunch today) sometimes we will surprisingly "feel everything becoming alright."

Just as there is no right or wrong way to grieve, there is no right or wrong way to experience special days without our loved one. The key is to genuinely experience them – in their imperfection, their pain, and their little surprises.

Tuning in to what Matters Most:

RIGHT THING:

- When it comes to holidays or special days, being prepared to tune in and genuinely acknowledge the feelings and emotions surrounding your family's loss is of utmost importance.

- Processing these emotions and planning for how we want these special days to be celebrated will help minimize the number of speed bumps we encounter.

- On these special days how can you prepare for emotions and reactions that you don't necessarily know are going to manifest, or what it will "look" like? The answer...we just have to do the best we can and believe that doing so will get us through. It is a learning process, it can be certainly be difficult, but with some experience we will get better at navigating these difficult days.

RIGHT TIME:

- The sooner you prepare for a holiday or special day the better. Greater preparation will result in fewer difficulties in managing the day. Again, it won't guarantee we don't hit bumps in the road, but it will help minimize the chances that we do.

- Affirm that all emotions you and your family members share are valid. Support the best you can, regroup, and then move on.

- The reality is that you have probably hit a few pot-holes already, and it is likely that you will run into more. The encouraging side to this is that each pot-hole serves as an opportunity to learn and develop your unique approach to navigating difficult times.

- Don't be afraid to try new approaches. Not all of them will work, but discovering what isn't helpful for your family has value as well. And sometimes, knowing what doesn't work can help you discover what does. As Thomas Edison once said: "I learned 10,000 ways not to make a light bulb."

RIGHT WAY:

- Having one or more family meetings prior to a holiday can be a good idea and a helpful way to anticipate any potentially difficult situations. Having one meeting early on (maybe a month or so out) and one a couple of days before the holiday will help you formalize an effective strategy for navigating your holiday season. What we think we want a month out may be different from what we realize we want as the day grows near. Changing the plan is ok; the key is to develop a strategy that your family can support and follow.

- This type of discussion should be held without distractions so that everyone can focus together. That means holding the meeting in the privacy of your home with no visitors around. Gather around the kitchen table or in another comfortable part of your home where you can sit face-to-face and really connect without the disruption of phones, iPads, TV and other distractions. To help you prepare for your family meeting, consider the following:

- Discuss emotional triggers; in other words, what needs to be avoided, what needs to be included to help avoid those emotional pot-holes?

- Acknowledge that the grieving process is difficult, normalize the feelings in your family, regroup so that you can learn from what works and what didn't, and then move on.

Holidays are always an opportunity to create family memories. Below are some suggestions for remembering loved ones during those special times.

- Create a memory collage using photos or magazine cut-outs of things that remind you of your loved one. Laminate your finished collage and use it as a placemat or wall hanging.

- Decorate a photo frame for your loved one's picture to and display it prominently.

- Create a "support chain" by linking strips of construction paper with memories of loved ones or other holidays or whatever you decide written on the strips.

- Write memories of special times with your loved ones on scraps of paper. Share them with one another and then place them in an ornament or decorative jar to leave out during the holidays.

- Cook your loved one's favorite meal and invite someone to share it with you.

- Light a special candle and create your own ritual. This could be sharing a favorite holiday memory, giving thanks for the blessings in your life, or asking for what you need.

CHAPTER 8

Grieving Men, Grieving Women

Myth: Women grieve more deeply than men.

Fact: Men grieve the loss of a loved one just as deeply as women, but they often experience and express the pain of loss differently.

"I didn't want to show my emotions in front of my sons because I'm a man, and men don't cry." – Geoff – **wife died of cancer, three sons, ages 12, 9, and 6**

"It was hard to talk about it...because, I feel like I failed. I didn't have the luxury of being vulnerable." – John, **14 year old daughter died suddenly, one son age 9, and one daughter age 6**

Just as adults often think children aren't grieving, because their grief doesn't look like adult grief, sometimes women think the men in their lives aren't grieving because they don't see their pain expressed in the same way.

Men and women, adults and children all feel the sharp, deep pain of the death of a loved one – but they express those feelings in very different ways.

In our Western, American culture men are often explicitly told not to cry – to think about something else, to squeeze their eyes shut, to look off into the distance – to do anything but let a tear fall. Women are freely given permission to cry, to show those harder emotions. When men and women are together grieving the same loss, it can feel lonely and confusing. Women often tend to want to talk about what happened and how they're feeling about the hard changes in their lives: the missing, the sadness, the anger and the pain. Men often shy away from talking about it; instead, they typically want to put their feelings into action – to do something. And, if they cry, they tend to do so alone.

The message that it's "unmanly" to express the pain that accompanies profound loss gets taught early in a boy's life.

Craig's Story:

For me, that lesson came at age 5 when my mother died, leaving behind my father and three small children: me and my two older siblings (ages 7 and 8 at the time). My dad was crushed by her death but he never let us see his grief. He soldiered on and expected everyone around him to do the same. He quickly went back to work and left us with a caretaker. When he came home, he never asked how I was doing and he certainly never shared what he was feeling. I was a boy and I was expected to learn from his example to be stoic. As a result, this defining event in all our lives was off limits for discussion. Our family took their cue from his behavior. "Be strong and don't cry. You need to be a man for your father." It didn't matter that what I needed most was someone to help me understand the fact that my mother was dead, and she was never coming back. My father had walled off his emotions and I soon learned that I needed to do the same. But in the process I became invisible, acutely aware that I was alone in feeling the weight of my mother's loss.

Fast forward many years to the recent death of a dear friend. Betty was a neighbor and the mother of a childhood buddy. After my mother passed away and all the relatives left, she quickly became a second mom to me. It was Betty who helped me to navigate the often confusing years after my father remarried, when I found myself living with a stepmother who had little time or energy to love a child that was not her "own." Betty and I kept in close contact even after I left home for college clear across the county. And even though I had seen her just weeks before her death and knew she was failing, I was totally blindsided by the flood of emotions I felt, yet tried to squelch, at her funeral. As I furiously fought back tears, I felt the same shame and vulnerability that my emotions were visible to others I had known as a child. And even though I have a loving family to support me, the messages of what it means to be a "man" haunted me. If I needed to be strong for others, how could I open up to share the burden of grief? Once again, I found myself alone, isolated and in pain.

In writing this, I know I'm not alone in these feelings. Our culture gives men mixed messages when it comes to death and loss. On the one hand, we expect men to suffer in silence; on the other hand, we judge them harshly as cold, distant and unfeeling when they appear not to be grieving fully. What a bind to be in! It's not surprising that so many men express their grief with what I call the 3 A's: action, anger and addiction.

Maybe you prefer to cry alone, or maybe you want a witness to your pain. Either way, it's important to give yourself permission to be vulnerable. If you don't find intentional ways to express your grief, you can't begin to heal.

For many men, putting feelings into action means creating a project in memory or honor of the person who died. Sometimes it means tearing apart the garage and reorganizing everything. One young man described his feelings in Grief Group as "jitter-buggy" – for him it felt like anxious over-activity, like he didn't know where to land.

One emotion that many men tend to find acceptable to express is anger. Judy Tatelbaum in The Courage to Grieve wrote, "Anger is our protest against that which cannot be changed." For men, it can feel more acceptable to punch a wall because you miss your loved one than it is to shed a tear. Taught to hide, deny, repress and avoid their feelings, men learn to fool themselves into believing they can power their way through grief. The problem is, eventually the "debt" comes due. Cut off from their feelings, it's common for men to shut up and shut down, distancing themselves from their remaining loved ones and their hearts. When this happens, complicated grief can set in, destroying their ability to enjoy life again. That grief may take the form of:

- Physical symptoms, such as headaches, fatigue, stomach problems and body aches.

- Substance abuse, addictive behavior and/or dependency.

- An increase in accidents.

- Chronic depression, irritability, and withdrawal.

- Indifference toward others, insensitivity and workaholism.

Navigating your way through grief

- Give yourself permission to experience your loss in your own way. Cry if you want to – it doesn't matter what others think.

- Give yourself time and space to mourn. Don't let others set a timetable for you.

- Allow yourself to slow down and focus on what you need.

- Build on this experience and use it to rebuild your life.

Supporting a man who is grieving

- Every man experiences grief in his own way. It's ok for men to grieve differently.

- Just because a man is silent doesn't mean he isn't mourning.

- Men tend to think their way through problems. Give them time to work through their feelings.

- Many men prefer time alone in order to heal.

- It's ok for men to feel and express anger, and not to cry. These are typical masculine responses to grief that may help them to heal.

- Be aware of special events and holidays and reach out to let your loved one know he's not alone.

- Gently encourage, but never push, your loved one to share his feelings. Telling someone how to grieve will only cause them to shut down emotionally, pushing them further into their pain.

Tuning in to what Matters Most:

RIGHT THING:

- Grief is a unique experience for every man and the way you grieve may not be what others expect or even what you expected of yourself. Yet all men and women need connection and empathy to work through their loss in healthy ways.

- Because of your gender, people may not see you as the bereaved person, but rather look to you to be stoic and strong. Don't confuse grieving with weakness. Find a safe place or someone to share your loss with who isn't afraid of your feelings and let your grief out. Holding in these strong emotions isn't healthy for you physically or emotionally. Feel whatever feelings wash over you and don't worry about what others think you should, or shouldn't, be doing.

RIGHT TIME:

- When a loved one dies, there are arrangements to be made, children to care for, and other mourners to attend to. It can be easy for men to fall into the support role, swallowing their own feelings in the process. While no man wants to shirk his duties, it's important to give yourself time to grieve. Let go of the mindset that you will focus on yourself after everything and everyone else is taken care of; your emotions and needs are every bit, if not more, important to you and the well-being of your family.

RIGHT WAY:

- When men experience loss, they tend to get overlooked. They're expected to be strong, to "suck up" and get on with things. However, when others fail to acknowledge their losses, men can feel isolated and misunderstood – and that can cause them to tamp down their grief even further. Sharing your grief and letting out your emotions, however difficult, is crucial to the healing process.

- Consider finding other men to talk with, especially those who have the personal experience and/or training to understand what you are going through. It can take courage and humility to admit you need help and to ask for it, but these connections can be some of your strongest sources of support and healing.

NOTES

CHAPTER 9

Special Circumstances...Talking About Suicide, Homicide, And Accidental Overdoses

Myth: Protect the children. Shield them from facts.

Fact: Children deserve to know the truth about how their loved one died. Present details age-appropriately, and with care.

"I don't know if I should tell them the truth, or if I even can." – **Cynthia who is now raising the 6 and 8 year-old children of her daughter, who died by suicide.**

Cynthia's story:

Cynthia came to the Grief Center hunched over, shuffling and wincing as she walked. Her young grandchildren trailed behind her silently with big, round eyes. The family was hurting. Cynthia told her grandchildren and the staff at the Grief Center that her daughter had died in a car accident the year before.

The day she died, Cynthia's daughter went to her children's school and called them out of class. She hugged them and said good bye. She then went home and hung herself. Hours after school let out, Cynthia came to pick up her grandchildren and took them to her house. The kids never again went back to the home they shared with their mother. Cynthia told everyone that her daughter had died in a car accident.

Slowly, a new pattern developed for the family. Little by little, both of the children began to shut down. They stopped talking in school. Her grandson got into a fistfight on the playground, but wouldn't say why or what happened. The school counselor called and was very concerned. She repeatedly encouraged Cynthia to attend the Grief Center, but Cynthia was afraid to take the kids to a place where they would talk about their mother's death. It took nearly a year after Cynthia's daughter died for the school counselor to get a crying Cynthia to call the Grief Center with her. Cynthia started bringing the kids to the Center. While the kids were each in their own Grief Group, listening to others who'd experienced death in their own families, Cynthia was in a group of her own. The first thing she asked her group was if she should tell her grandchildren how their mother had really died.

As weeks and then months passed, Cynthia found the words and the strength to tell the children what had really happened to their mom. They seemed to have already known. It wasn't as hard as she had thought. Nearly imperceptibly, the whole family started to shift. Cynthia started walking without pain and standing taller. The kids started to share in group. They practiced talking about their mom and telling their stories. They began to smile. Finally, they even started to laugh again.

Several years after the family closed from group and went on their own way, I ran into the oldest child. She had just started 8th grade and was positively bubbly with all of the excitement in her life. I asked her how she was doing and she said, "Well, last month was Mom's birthday, so we made her favorite dinner – spaghetti! And we told stories about her. We talked about what we missed. We talked about what we wished was different. She was a great mom, but she didn't know how to handle her pain sometimes. Still, we made it a good birthday!"

Giving the hard news that someone has died:

Just as we explain any other death to children, we start by concretely defining what has happened. We always tell the truth in an age-appropriate way, which allows us to build a foundation of trust. Details can come later. Questions can, and will, come later as well.

To begin with, we say that someone has died. For very young children, we have to explain the difference between alive and dead. We have to explain that once someone has died, they cannot breathe, think, walk, talk or feel. They can't come back to us. We will miss them for a long, long time. Again, we must first operationally define that someone has died, and explain the difference between being alive and dead. As fundamental as it sounds, it's important to define the language we use like "died" before we introduce our beliefs about afterlife or anything else.

When telling a young person that someone they love has died, take your time. Allow for silence. Allow for questions. It's ok to say, "I don't know the answer to that, but I will help you find out."

Telling kids someone they loved died by suicide:

At the Grief Center, we are careful to say "died by suicide" as opposed to "committed suicide." When someone dies by suicide, we say they were hurting so much that this was the only way they knew to stop the pain. They had a very specific kind of illness in the brain – mental illness – and the illness made it impossible for them to think clearly and to get the help they needed.

A death by suicide is sudden. It's unexpected. Everyone is in shock. If you don't say everything you wanted to the first time you talk about the death, you can go back and do it again. It's ok to bring it up. Everyone is thinking about it anyway, even if they try to act like they're not.

It's important to emphasize – no matter what the situation – that the special person who died did not choose to leave their loved ones behind and that they never intended to hurt their loved ones. It's also very important to emphasize that when someone is determined to die by suicide, there is no amount of love that can stop them. To quote Donna Schuurman, Executive Director of The

Dougy Center in Portland, Oregon: "Love alone does not and cannot prevent suicide, any more than it can prevent cancer or car crashes. People who are suicidal are in severe emotional pain, and hopelessness takes over their ability to imagine possible routes out of the pain, other than death."

Special concerns in surviving a suicide death:

- **Is it genetic or contagious?** Children who are related to someone who dies by suicide need to be reassured that this is not their fate as well. It's ok to say, "Your (mom/dad/brother) had a very serious mental illness, but this does not mean anyone else in our family has to die this way. There are doctors and medications that can help. The key is to talk about it, to ask for help, and to know that dying isn't the only solution to pain."

- **Stigma.** Try to connect with others who've survived the suicide of a loved one. Support groups and Internet sites abound with people who have walked this path before you. There are numerous detailed, helpful books on the subject (check the Resources section of this book). Most people will not understand the many, powerfully strong emotions and questions that accompany a loved one's suicide. Rumors will abound.

- **Faith.** Most deaths challenge our faith. Many Catholics, for example, believe that if someone took their own life, their souls are doomed for eternity. The 1994 publication of <u>Catechism of the Catholic Church</u> says the suicide breaks the natural path of life, but that the church will pray for those who died by suicide.

- **Guilt.** Survivors of a loved one's suicide may ask themselves what they could have done to save them. The answer is, nothing. If someone is determined to die by suicide, they will. Connect with other survivors who understand this pain. Children will often feel they did or said something that caused their loved one to die. Bring this up directly and remind them that they are not responsible for their loved one's death.

Telling kids someone they love died by homicide:

The fact is that someone important in this child's life is gone. That is the first and foremost issue. The "how" it happened can be given in small doses appropriate for the child's age and understanding.

When someone we love dies and it is the fault of someone else's actions – be it accidental or with intent – it can be easy to focus the anger, rage and hurt on the other person. Seeking vengeance or justice can occupy so much of the survivors' lives that they lose focus on the loved ones left in it. Sitting in a courtroom and hearing the details of your loved one's last moments, even watching the person responsible receive a severe punishment, won't make the pain go away. That can be another great loss and very hard to accept.

Special concerns following a homicide:

- **Stigma.** Many people believe that if someone is murdered, they must have had it coming to them somehow/someway.

- **Fear.** The reality that someone we love can die at the hand of someone else can make the world feel like a very scary place. It's important to emphasize all that is done/will be done to keep the other people in the family safe. Homicide, as much as we hear about it in American media and even when it occurs in our own families, is a relatively rare way to die. Yet, children who experience any manner of death are hyper-sensitive to the fact that everyone they love can and will die eventually. Reassure them that there will always be someone to take care of them.

- **Revenge.** Father Richard Rohr once said, "Pain that is not transformed, is transmitted." The idea that hurting the person who hurt us will somehow mitigate our pain is an old and outdated idea. It does not work. We have to mourn the person we lost and re-invest in life.

- **Guilt.** "If only..." Survivors of a loved one's homicide can replay the moments before their lives changed forever and see many things they could have/should have done. Nothing can change what happened. However, we can change how we go forward into each new day. Children will often feel they did or said something that caused their loved one to die. Bring this up directly – remind them that they are not responsible for their loved one's death.

- **Media.** If the circumstances around the death of your loved one are suddenly played out on the nightly news, in the paper or in social media, it can feel inescapable. Often, media accounts get the details wrong. Sometimes, they portray the person we loved in an unflattering light. Sometimes, they invade your space. It is ok to say "No" to reporters. You can't correct all the misinformation in the world, but you can let the young people in your life know that it's out there. "There will be rumors, there will be stories and questions about this death. We don't have to respond to them unless we feel ready."

Telling kids someone they love died by accidental overdose:

Please, take a moment to read through the sections on Suicide and Homicide. Accidental Overdose is a death that seems to lie between those two experiences.

An accidental overdose can occur when someone we love has had a known struggle with addiction, and sometimes it can occur because someone just mixed the wrong medications. Sometimes we don't know what or how it happened.

Special concerns in an overdose death:

- **Addiction.** If substance abuse runs in the family, talk about getting extra help – from school counselors or other trusted adults.

- **Guilt.** The "would have/should haves" can take over. Nothing can change what happened. We can change how we go forward into each new day. Children will often feel they did or said something that caused their loved one to die. Bring this up directly and remind them that they are not responsible for their loved one's death.

In all of these sudden losses, there isn't time to say goodbye. That can be an on-going struggle for survivors. Your conversation with your loved one was cut short. When you are ready, and it may be sometime after the memorial or funeral services, you can take time out to say a special goodbye. There are many ways to include the young people in the family. Write a message on a balloon and send it up into the sky, write messages on paper and burn them in a special fire. Talk to a picture or other tangible representation of your loved one. And just because you do it once, doesn't mean you can't do it again if you need to.

Tuning in to what Matters Most:

RIGHT THING:

- When someone close to you dies by suicide, homicide, or overdose, your grief may be intensified because such a loss can be difficult to comprehend. The right thing is to pay attention and tune into your emotions as a first step toward understanding them.

- You may experience intense feelings of shock, anger and guilt. You may feel despondent, even desperate to go back and wish for another outcome. Notice when you are feeling washed over by grief and give yourself quiet time and space to heal.

RIGHT TIME:

- Shock is a common reaction to death, especially one that is sudden and unexpected. You may feel numb for a few days, a few weeks, or even longer.

- Take some time to be alone, if that's what you want and need, but be careful not to isolate yourself. Return to your own life and routine as soon as you feel ready.

RIGHT WAY:

- The right way to handle this type of loss is by giving yourself permission to feel whatever feelings you have and to process them in whatever way works for you.

- These feelings may overwhelm you at first, but trust that you can handle and move past them with time. Try to understand and accept that your emotions are normal, healthy and a painful but necessary part of the healing process.

NOTES

NOTES

CHAPTER 10

Finding A New Way To Feel Normal Again

> Myth: Time heals all wounds.
>
> Fact: "The medicine of time, taken by itself, is not sure. Time is neutral. What helps is what you do with time." – Rabbi Earl Grollman

"The Grief Center got us to the point….we live our life. We love like nobody's business. We enjoy each day." **Mark, father of 3, wife died of leukemia**

<u>Mark's Story:</u>

"When my wife died, I was a train wreck. We had three boys. They were 12, 8 and 6 at the time. She was sick for a year. We knew she was going to die. It was just crazy. They said goodbye, and then it was like everything fell apart. What had kept us going – being there through her illness – just stopped when she did. The oldest was drawing pictures of shooting himself. The middle one was hiding under his desk at school, holding onto a blanket she had given him. The youngest was getting picked on at school – he was vulnerable – he was a target. I couldn't sleep, and I didn't want to cry in front my sons because I'm a man, and I didn't think that was an ok example to set for them. We were lost, numb. We found our way to the Grief Center. After the first night, I asked the boys "What'd you think of it?" and they said 'They're like us Dad, they're like us.' I was in a group of women who'd lost their husbands, and we learned about our grief together. The kids would play, they'd share their story, and slowly we started to be able to talk about her in our groups and then together. A few years have passed now. The Grief Center got us to the point....we live our life. We love like nobody's business. We enjoy each day."

The moment you hear the news that someone you love has died, your world is never the same. The first few days streak by with arrangements to be made, well wishers visiting, a kind of surreal numbness settles over everything. Some of us respond by diving into the busyness, like a spinning top – if we stop spinning, we fall down. Others retreat from the world, denying the reality of the loss, pushing away the horrible decisions and tasks that come along with death.

It's hard to imagine ever feeling normal or ok again – and in a way – you won't. You will be forever shaped by this experience. Profound grief changes us. Part of our work is to recognize those changes, and to become ok with them.

There are many who have walked this grief journey before you. They know the immediate, wrenching pain of the loss. They know the slow ache that never fully subsides. They know that even as years pass, the process of reconciling the loss of a loved one into our ongoing lives can often feel like resignation. They know it's so hard to believe now – but there is a future for you and your family. It can even be a beautiful future.

We asked several families like Mark's who've been through the death of a partner or child to share their thoughts. This is what they had to say.

<u>Things I want newly bereaved parents to know:</u>

- You are going to survive this.

- You learn to love a whole lot better, stronger, differently.

- You learn not to take anyone for granted. You learn the value of your loved ones. You learn that life is not guaranteed.

- You get accustomed to being uncomfortable.

- You do some nutty things when you're grieving. Your kids do some nutty things too – meet them at the place they are.

- You have to learn what your "new normal" is and remember you're not setting the table for the same number of people anymore.

- You need to tell the kids: It's ok if I cry. I'm crying because I loved him/her. They (the kids) are not making me cry.

The first year after my loved one died...

- I felt like a walking ghost.

- I don't know how I got through it.

- Grieving isn't done in a year, it's not done in three years, not done in six.

- I have a need to keep my life "neater." I think about what I will leave behind if I die suddenly.

- We talk about kids regressing, but even adults revert to comforting or immature behaviors.

- I learned not to be controlled by someone else just because they're "experts." You've got to pay attention to your own intuition about what is right for your kids/family.

At the Grief Center, we sometimes encounter children, teens, even adults who have identified so closely with the pain of their loss, they become very comfortable dwelling in their own personal valley of the shadow. They may feel guilt or shame if they were to laugh or enjoy themselves – as if experiencing life more fully again would disrespect the memory of the person who died, or dishonor their own experience of grieving that loss.

In <u>A Grief Observed</u>, C.S. Lewis wrote, "Getting over a painful experience is much like crossing the monkey bars – you have to let go at some point to move forward."

Not sure how to let go to move forward? We can learn from the youngest children in our families. They experience the pain of the loss – they pause, recognize, feel the hard feelings – and then they continue on. This may happen a few times a day, or a few times a week. Eventually the times between those sharp points of painful grief will expand and fill with what has become your new life. It takes care, it takes honoring those experiences, and it takes the courage to let them go. Like everything else on this journey, it will happen at a different pace for the different members of your family.

A young mother of three children ages 2, 6, and 10 was visited by police chaplains bearing the news that her husband had just been killed in a motorcycle accident. She brought her family to the Children's Grief Center, and they were able to participate in peer support groups, share their stories, and learn from others. Over the course of a few years, the children grew up, and they grew strong. They were able to talk about their father clearly with joy and with sadness, to recognize the experience of his loss in their lives and to move in and out of the hard feelings that accompany grief. Eventually, their mother fell in love again with a wonderful man. Speaking publicly about their experience for the first time she said, "The Grief Center allowed us to step into the life that was waiting for us."

Whether or not you have a place like the Children's Grief Center in your town, you have a community. You have these stories. You have resources in the back of this book where you can connect virtually to others who share experiences like yours. You are not alone. You are "stronger than you believe and braver than you think" to paraphrase that great sage, Winnie the Pooh. There is a life waiting for you. We promise.

Additional Resources

Additional Resources

INTERNET

- Hello Grief. An online support community for teens: www.hellogrief.org

- National Alliance for Grieving Children: www.childrengrieve.org

- The Children's Grief Center of New Mexico: www.childrensgrief.org

- Support for widowers whose wife died of cancer: www.singlefathers-duetocancer.org

- Comfort Zone Camp: A national camp for grieving young people: www.comfortzonecamp.org

- The Compassionate Friends: Worldwide site for Compassionate Friends, a support group for parents who have lost children:www.compassionatefriends.org

- The Dougy Center:www.dougy.org

- Suicide loss www.suicidefindinghope.com

BOOKS FOR YOUNG CHILDREN THAT ADDRESS GRIEF & LOSS

- Saying Goodbye to Daddy by Judith Vigna

- <u>The Tenth Good Thing About Barney</u> by Judith Viorst

- <u>Tell the Paper</u>, a Centering Corporation Resource

- <u>The Fall of Freddie the Leaf</u> by Leo Buscaglia

- <u>Healing Your Grieving Heart: 100 Practical Ideas for Kids</u> by Alan D. Wolfelt, PhD

- <u>Lifetimes: the Beautiful way to Explain Death to Children</u> Bryan Mellonie and Robert Ingpen

- <u>When Someone Very Special Dies, Children Can Learn to Cope with Grief</u> by Marge Heegaard

- <u>Badger's Parting Gifts</u> by Susan Varley

BOOKS FOR PRE-TEENS

- <u>Crossing 13 – Memoir of a Father's Suicide</u> by Carrie Stark Hugus

- <u>After You Lose Someone You Love – Advice and Insight from the Diaries of 3 Kids Who've Been There</u> as told by Dave, Allie and Amy Dennison

- <u>A Sister's Diary</u> by Jodi Scheinfeld (based on a true story)

- <u>Help for Getting Through the Hard Times: Getting Through Loss</u> by Earl Hipp

- <u>Tear Soup: A Recipe for Healing After Loss</u> by Pat Schwiebert

BOOKS FOR TEENS

- <u>What Jamie Saw</u> by Carolyn Coman

- <u>Healing Your Grieving Heart for Teens</u> by Alan D. Wolfelt, PhD

- <u>Teenagers Face to Face with Bereavement</u> by Karen Gravelle and Charles Haskins

- <u>Death is Hard to Live With: Teenagers Talk about How They Cope with Loss</u> by Janet Bode

- <u>How It Feels When a Parent Dies</u> by Jill Krementz

- <u>You Are Not Alone: Teens Talk About Life After Loss of a Parent</u> by Lynne B. Hughes

BOOKS FOR ADULTS ON CHILDHOOD BEREAVEMENT

- <u>The Seasons of Grief: Helping Children Grow Through Loss</u> by Donna A. Gaffney

- <u>Why did Daddy Die? Helping Children Cope With the Loss of a Parent</u> by Linda Alderman

- <u>Helping Children Cope with the Loss of a Loved One: A Guide for Grownups</u> by William Kroen, PhD, LMHC

- <u>A Child's View of Grief</u> by Alan D. Wolfelt, PhD

- <u>On Children and Death</u> by Elisabeth Kubler-Ross

- <u>Children Mourning, Mourning Children</u>, Edited by Kenneth J. Doka, PhD

- <u>I Wasn't Ready To Say Good-Bye</u> by Brook Noel and Pamela D. Blair, PhD

- <u>Nobody's Child Anymore: Grieving, Caring and Comforting When Parents Die</u> by Barbara Bartocci

- <u>Safe Passage: Words to Help the Grieving Hold Fast and Let Go</u> by Molly Fumia

- <u>Death, Loss and Grief in Literature for Youth: A Selective Annotated Bibliography for K-12</u> by Alice Crosetto and Rajinder Garcha

BOOKS FOR ADULTS ON GRIEF & LOSS

- <u>Surviving Grief…And Learning to Live Again</u> by Catherine M. Sanders, PhD

- <u>When Bad Things Happen to Good People</u> by Harold S. Kushner

- <u>A Grief Observed</u> by C. S. Lewis

- <u>Healing After Loss: Daily Meditations for Working Through Grief</u> by Martha Whitmore Hickman

- <u>When People Grieve: The Power of Love in the Midst of Pain</u> by Paula D'Arcy

About The Authors

Jade Richardson Bock

Jade Richardson Bock is the Executive Director of the Children's Grief Center of New Mexico. The Children's Grief Center (www.childrensgrief.org) provides support groups for children, teens and young adults ages 5 - 25 coping with the death of a caregiver or a sibling. Ms. Bock grew up in southern Virginia on her family's commercial peach orchard. Her father was killed in an accident when she was 17. She continued to manage successful for-profit businesses until coming to CGC first as a volunteer bereavement facilitator in 2003, than as an employee in 2005. Under her leadership the Center has more than quadrupled the number of families served, volunteers engaged, and dollars raised to provide free support groups for grieving young people.

Dr. Craig Pierce

Craig Pierce, PhD is the Founder and President of Southwest Family Guidance Center and Institute, and the creator of the Attunetion Approach*. With more than 30 years of mental health experience, Dr. Pierce is a fellow with the American Psychotherapy Association, working extensively in the public school system and in private practice as a school counselor and psychologist, and as a clinical director. His specialty areas of treatment include family therapy, domestic abuse, sexual and childhood abuse, childhood disorders, interpersonal neurobiology and clinical supervision.

Made in the USA
San Bernardino, CA
19 June 2015